Smiles and Blessings

For…

May God bless you richly
and give you 10,000 reasons
to smile!

From…

D1380605

The LORD has done great things for us,
and we are filled with joy.

Psalms 126:3
New International Version

Start the day with a smile!

Did you know it takes around
12 facial muscles to smile?
So, smile often – it's great exercise!
And, happily, everyone smiles in
the same language!

•

This is the day the LORD has made.
Let's rejoice and be glad today!

Psalm 118:24
GOD'S WORD Translation

Jonathan Leach, Sunflowers

3

Smile! God created you!

You are chosen.
You are special.
You are unique.
You are God's masterpiece.

•

God looked at everything he had made,
and he was very pleased.

Genesis 1:31
Good News Translation

Smile! God delights in you!

The LORD your God
is with you;
his power gives you victory.
The LORD will take
delight in you,
and in his *love* he will
give you new life.
He will sing and be
joyful over you...

Zephaniah 3:17
Good News Translation

6

Smile! God is good!

There is so much to be thankful for.

•

The LORD has done great things for us,
and we are filled with joy.

Psalm 126:3
New International Version

•

Be strengthened by the faith
that you were taught,
and overflow with thanksgiving.

Colossians 2:7
GOD'S WORD Translation

Jonathan Leach, Clifton, Bristol

Smile! It's a wonderful world!

Let the heavens rejoice and the earth be happy!
Let the sea and everything in it shout for joy!
Let the fields and everything in them be happy!
Let the trees in the forest sing for joy
when they see the LORD coming!

Psalm 96:11–13
Easy-to-Read Version

•

The power of finding beauty in the humblest things
makes home happy and life lovely.

Louisa May Alcott
American novelist, 1832–1888

Charles Kinsey, Madagascar

Shout for Joy to the LORD,
all the earth.

Psalm 100:1
New International Version

The be-attitudes

Be happy
Be joyful
Be thankful
Be thoughtful
Be enthusiastic
Be positive
Be patient
Be gentle
Be kind

•

Blessed are the pure in heart,
for they shall see God.

Matthew 5:8
World English Bible

A smile can...

Break the ice,
Bridge the gap,
Brighten a dull day,
Reassure a friend,
Welcome a stranger,
and
Help everyone feel included.

•

Smile, for everyone lacks self-confidence
and more than any other one thing
a smile reassures them.

André Maurois
French author, 1885-1967

14

How slight a nod it would take, how bare a smile,
to give everyone you meet today a sense of worth.

Robert Brault
American author

SMILE

See Miracles In

Life Every day

15

A smile is...

A smile is happiness you'll find right under your nose.

Tom Wilson
American cartoonist, 1931–2011

A smile is a curve that sets everything straight.

Phyllis Diller
American comedian, 1917–2012

A smile is a powerful weapon
– you can even break ice with it...

A smile is wonderful therapy.

A smile is free but it's worth a lot.

A smile is priceless

Don't underestimate all the good
that a simple smile can do.
Making someone smile can change the world.
Maybe not the whole world, but their world.
So, be the reason someone smiles today
and improve the world, one smile at a time.

●

A body smiles, like, 72 times a day.
Where does that smile go?
That's what I want to know.

Goldie Hawn
American actress, 1945-present day

The real question

Did I offer peace today?
Did I bring a smile to someone's face?
Did I say words of healing?
Did I let go of my anger and resentment?
Did I forgive?
Did I love?
These are the real questions.
I must trust that the little bit of love that I sow now
will bear many fruits,
here in this world and the life to come.

Henri Nouwen
Dutch Catholic priest and theologian, 1932–1996

Wise Words

Every time you smile at someone,
it is an action of love,
a gift to that person,
a beautiful thing.

...

Be the living expression of
God's kindness;
kindness in your face,
kindness in your eyes,
kindness in your smile.

...

Peace begins with a smile.

Mother Teresa
Catholic nun and missionary, 1910-1997

Now may the Lord of peace himself give you
peace at all times and in every way.
The Lord be with all of you.

2 Thessalonians 3:16
New International Version

Jonathan Leach, Spring lamb

23

Smile often

Laugh loudly
Love others
Dream big
Spread joy
Have hope
Praise God
Seize the day
And never, NEVER take life for granted.

•

Smiling is infectious,
You can catch it like the flu.
Someone smiled at me today,
And I started smiling too.

Jez Alborough
English writer, 1959–present

Awesome Advice

Your smile is your logo,
your trademark,
your character.
Your smile is what makes you YOU.
Practise it often.

•

Wear a smile and have friends;
wear a scowl and have wrinkles.

George Eliot
English novelist, 1819-1880

Christ works through you

Christ has no body now but yours.
No hands, no feet on earth but yours.
Yours are the eyes through which
he looks compassion on this world.
Yours are the feet with which he walks to do good.
Yours are the hands through which
he blesses all the world.
Yours are the hands, yours are the feet,
yours are the eyes,
You are his body.
Christ has no body now on earth but yours.

Saint Teresa of Avila
Spanish Saint, 1515-1582

Always pray to have
eyes that see the
best in people,
a heart that forgives
the worst,
a mind that forgets
the bad, and
a soul that
never loses faith
in God.

Anon

The value of a single smile

Smiling is free,
Smiling is contagious,
Smiling improves our mood.
Smiling makes life more beautiful,
Smiling makes us look more attractive,
Smiling exercises the face muscles.
Smiling makes us feel younger,
Smiling encourages others,
Smiling relieves stress.

SMILE – just because you can!

Doctors say that smiling
can reduce blood pressure,
increase endurance,
reduce pain, relieve stress
and strengthen your
immune system.

Wow! How many more reasons do you need?

The importance of a single smile

A smile costs nothing, but gives much.
It enriches those who receive
without making poorer those who give.
It takes but a moment,
but the memory of it sometimes lasts forever.
None is so rich or mighty that he cannot get along
without it and none is so poor
that he cannot be made rich by it.
Yet a smile cannot be bought, begged, borrowed,
or stolen, for it is something that is of no value
to anyone until it is given away.

Some people are too tired to give you a smile.
Give them one of yours, as none needs a smile
so much as he who has no more to give.

Inspired by *The Value of a Smile* by Dale Carnegie,
adapted and updated by unknown author.

May God smile on you

May God have pity on us and bless us!
May he smile on us.

Psalm 67:1
GOD'S WORD Translation

•

May the light of God's love shine into your life
this week so that you have more than enough
to share it with others.

May God give you hope

May the God of hope fill you with all joy
and peace as you trust in him,
so that you may overflow with hope
by the power of the Holy Spirit.

Romans 15:13
New International Version

•

The LORD is trustworthy in all he promises
and faithful in all he does.

Psalm 145:13
New International Version

May God change every frown to a smile

I went to the LORD for help,
and he listened.
He saved me from all that I fear.
If you look to him for help,
he will put a smile on your face.

Psalm 34:4-5
Easy-to-Read Version

May God bless you

May God bless you richly today
and fill your life with love and joy.
I pray that he'll put his peace in your heart,
his wisdom in your mind and
his smile on your face.

•

May you be blessed by the LORD,
the Maker of heaven and earth.

Psalm 115:15
New International Version

40

Some people count money, some count steps,
and others count calories –
why not stop and count your blessings instead?

May God fill your life with joy

The LORD is my strength and my shield;
my heart trusts in him, and he helps me.
My heart leaps for joy,
and with my song I praise him.

Psalm 28:7
New International Version